AN INSIDER'S GUIDE ON HOW TO SELL YOUR BUSINESS

A Broker's Perspective

CHRISTINA LAZURIC WOSCOFF

This book is dedicated to the brave souls that dared to be their own boss and the masters of their own destiny. Creating and running your own business can be a long and lonely road. There were probably days when you wanted to throw in the towel, but you didn't, you stuck it out. Now you have something worthy of passing on.

You and your business matter to the people that you work with, in addition to all the lives that have been affected along the way. When you're ready to pass the torch, do it right. Do not have regrets because the best is yet to come! The same passion that once drove your business forward is ready to emerge into something new.

Contents

Disclaimer

The information provided in this guide does not constitute legal, tax or accounting advice, but is designed to provide general information relating to business and commerce. California Business Brokers Inc. content, information products and services are not a substitute for obtaining the advice of a competent professional, for example a licensed attorney, law firm, accountant or financial adviser.

Acknowledgements

I WOULD LIKE TO THANK MY DAUGHTER, VANESSA, WHO ASSISTED IN THE EARLIER editing drafts and gave sound feedback, as well as assisting with the title of the book.

I would like to thank my long-time friend Darleen Sweet for her insights into the bulk sale escrow process.

I would like to thank my friend and a previous client Lisa Sutton who actually went through the process of selling her business with me years ago and was a great source of checks and balances in the book.

Lastly, I thank my husband Leo who puts up with me, listens to my ideas, and generally encourages me at all times to keep moving forward.

Introduction

My name is Christina Lazuric Woscoff, I am principal and broker of California Business Brokers Inc., I have been a business broker since 2005. I'm originally from Montreal, Canada but I have lived in beautiful Orange County, California since 1999. My brokerage has facilitated the transfer of over 300 local businesses, resulting in hundreds of millions of dollars worth of closed deals.

At the tender age of 24 I owned my first ever business, a baby clothing manufacturer called Babetex. My very first sale was to a small chain, and boy I was impressed with myself. I'm pretty sure my feet hovered above the ground from pure joy at my first big purchase order. What I didn't know was that in 45 days she would announce her impending bankruptcy—not good times. I was naive in giving her terms that I really couldn't afford, but I did. So, when she started closing her locations I tracked her down and begged her to pay me. I was very fortunate that she took pity on me and paid me in the end. In the grand scheme of everything I think back to that time, and I believe that she knew that she would just crush me as a young entrepreneur if she hadn't kept her end of the deal. I was a single mom back then and this was the last few dollars I had in the world, it would have been pretty cold of her had she not paid me. Anyway, children's clothing isn't like ladies clothing, they don't allow many in a shopping center. There is usually one national chain plus one other small chain or boutique. When I found out she was closing, I also found out that her best store was going to close, it couldn't support the others that were bringing it down. Once the dust settled, I contacted the shopping center and leased a space from them. Although I had a clever idea, I made the critical mistake of not insisting on the same location in the shopping center as the one that had just closed. They sold me a store that was on the second floor, but they offered me a better price on the rent and free rent while it was being built out. I learned the first rule in both real estate and business: location, location, location. The second floor was terrible, it never received the same volume of traffic as the first floor. I worked very hard in that business, but two years later I closed it. It sounds like a failure, but in reality, it was the greatest lesson I ever had. I learned many important things from that experience that carried me throughout my whole life. I learned how to negotiate, secure terms with vendors, work with architects and contractors, pick merchandise, hire and manage employees, advertise, deal with customers and landlords—and more. That experience was over 30 years ago, and I am still grateful today for all that I learned from it, there are no failures in business if you can take away a lesson learned from it.

After trying it on my own, I decided it was time to provide a stable income for my family, so I took a corporate job for a fortune 500 company and started climbing the ladder. I worked there for 10 years and I was promoted several times, but it was never my intention to stay, so I accepted a transfer from Montreal, Canada to California, and never looked back.

I started selling businesses because I owned a small business in Orange County, a dollar store, and I had a devil of a time finding a competent broker to represent me. After a year of trying, and going through two brokers, I eventually found a mentor and sold it myself, which is not something I normally recommend. My mentor convinced me that the combination of my own entrepreneurial background and my corporate management experience would make me an ideal business broker. He was right of course, I took to it right away. I found myself able to connect with both the sellers and the buyers. I immediately realized that even though I'm selling businesses, the transactions are totally personal to everyone involved, and there are a lot of emotions running deep on both sides. Once you attune yourself to that fact, it's easier to handle the emotions that people display during these deals. If you think about the amount of time in your precious life that's gone into the business you've built, it's no wonder sellers feel so emotional about it. My journey as an entrepreneur had ups and downs, even after the sale. About two months after we closed escrow on my business that I sold, I received a call from the buyer, who was a wonderful person that bought the business for his son to run—and his son was thrilled to have it. The buyer called me and said, "Christina you better sit down. No one got hurt but the whole business just burned down to the ground." After my initial shock, I shed a few tears when I thought of all the time I had spent trying to make that place special. I was so happy to think it would live on past me, and have a life of its own, but now it was completely gone—as if it had never existed—I was very sad. It had nothing to do with the money, that wasn't in the equation. It was pure sentiment. So, when a seller is sizing up a buyer that I've brought in, he/she is wondering if this person is going to take good care of the baby they raised. I wouldn't have been able to relate to that fact if I hadn't owned my own business and gone through similar experiences myself.

I really do my best to prepare both sides for what is likely to happen, and that's the reason I wrote this book. However, it's impossible to prepare for all eventualities. There are so many moving parts to a business that you should always expect the unexpected. I do my best to be the calm force that gets all the moving parts in line, and maintain a good and cooperative relationship between the buyer and seller. I know that the business being sold is much more than just a business, it's your legacy and it deserves to be treated as such.

Prologue

A FEW THINGS YOU NEED TO KNOW ABOUT THIS BOOK. FIRST, THE BUSIEST people I know are entrepreneurs. The reason for that is because business owners often wear many hats: accountant, human resources, marketing, sometimes even janitor! That is the reason this book is written without any filler. I have read countless self-help types of books that are full of fluff and lack any true substance. I'm not going to build you up throughout 150 pages simply to tell you what you need to know in the final 50 pages. At first you were probably thinking to yourself, *"Wow this book seems a little smaller than other books."* Well, you're right, and that's because I get right to the point about the things you need to know as a potential seller. This book is not meant to prepare you to sell your business yourself, if you really want to take that on then you're reading the wrong book. I truly believe in letting professionals do what they do best. Most people are smart enough to see the value of letting someone who knows what to do handle the impossible scenarios that can occur. I repeat often in the book to expect the unexpected, I'm saying it here, in print, that it is 100% true! I've learned never to count on a potential paycheck because it isn't done until escrow is closed, and until then anything can happen.

This book is a guide, or a tool that will give you a better understanding of what can be done to sell your business for the best and highest price, as quickly as possible, based on well over a dozen years of experience.

Second, this is not a dry text book. It's written in a format that people can relate to, and it's even a little humorous. Perhaps my perspective is different because I was you at some point, and I just wanted someone to explain what I could do to sell my business. That's what I've done in this book.

Lastly, I have included many unbelievable (but true) interesting stories from both sellers and buyers that I've encountered over the years. I have always said that I really could not make up all the situations that have occurred during my deals. I was approached about three times to do a reality show, and when you read through all my stories I'm sure you'll understand why.

I have been told that I can be blunt at times. I find I'm blunt with the people I am closest to, and that I respect the most. It's a disservice not to tell people what they need to hear if you have a) been asked, and b) have the necessary experience and some authority on the subject. If you are anything like me then you just want to know how to fix the problem and achieve your goal. Everything I'm going to lay out for you in this guide should help you to sell your business. That doesn't mean that every business will sell. In addition to factors such as organized books and records, cash flow, strategic management in place and all the other common-sense steps we are going to cover, there is one important factor that is often overlooked: desirability. I was once in a meeting with a motorcycle manufacturer, and I asked him why he wanted to sell his lucrative business. He said, *"Because I'm tired of getting a report every other week about someone who died using my product."* I had to admit that he had a point, not everything is about money.

Over all these years of selling businesses I've learned that some of them just won't sell, even if I think they should. These are businesses with clean books and consistent profit. In those cases, it is almost always because of the catch 22 issue. They are not big enough to attract the right buyer, but they are also too big to attract the right buyer. I'll give you an example. I had a listing for a commercial air conditioning company and they hit many markers that I look for. They had been in business for over 18 years, they had consistent income, simple unencumbered tax returns, their equipment was in decent shape and they had a steady staff. Fast forward to two years later, I couldn't sell it, and to my knowledge it never sold. Here's the reason, first it's a business that requires skill and a specific license to own. Imagine thousands of buyers swimming in a pool. Businesses valued at under a million dollars have different buyers than larger businesses that sell for 2 million or more. Many of the smaller businesses are purchased by the masses: people who are new to the United States, people who have been let go by their employment and need something new to do, people who have been forced into an early retirement but still want to work etc. So, let's take out all the swimmers who are not interested or capable of getting a license to own and operate an air conditioning company. Now there are very few people left in the pool. In addition, most of the people left in the pool don't have adequate financial resources to purchase a million-dollar business. To recap, you need skill and a license, and you need to be financially capable of purchasing a million-dollar listing. It's way too big for a technician who wants to become his own boss, but it's too small for a conglomerate to acquire in order to fold into their portfolio. In this case I suggested a different kind of exit strategy, perhaps a narrow-focused succession plan involving his network of employees and/or competitors. This is what's called a strategic buyer, we'll cover that later in another chapter.

Here's the bottom line: when people ask me how long it will take to sell their business I use this analogy: it's like going on a dating website and trying to choose the right partner. If you're gorgeous, skinny, intelligent and financially secure it shouldn't take any time at all. If you're overweight, unattractive, dim-witted and broke, it might take a while. I'm your personal trainer and I'll do the best I can to make you as lovely and attractive as possible to get you sold, but I'm not a miracle worker. Stay real about the business that you're selling and try to disregard your emotions when stating what you "feel" it's worth. While everyone who has ever owned a business feels your pain on sweat equity, buyers don't care about your late nights and spoiled weekends. They care about desirability and cash flow.

Case Study 1.

A few years ago, I sold a very profitable and desirable janitorial company that specialized in cleaning a specific type of business. It had been in business for many years and had strong steady growth, with clean books and records. This business was classified as service-based, supplying other businesses (B2B), which makes it very valuable. Some people have trouble understanding that part. They think that if the business transfers with a lot of expensive assets it's a good deal, when in fact assets are only a minor consideration. The company sold for over a million dollars, and all I transferred was a bunch of vacuum cleaners. What made it valuable was that it had very little fixed overhead, so it could remain profitable under almost any circumstance. When a buyer purchases a business they always think of the 'worst case scenario.' Businesses that have a lot of fixed expenses, like high rent, equipment leases and payroll are riskier, because in the worst-case scenario you could be hit hard on a monthly basis and drain your resources. In addition, buyers favor businesses that service the business sector rather than the public. In theory, dealing with other companies is easier than dealing with the public. Another valuable element was the fact that it was a niche. Niche businesses are always highly appreciated by buyers because they are more difficult to come by. Finally, it had an even distribution of accounts, so no one account represented over 15% of the gross income. Lastly, they had reoccurring revenue which is the ultimate check in a buyer's box of pluses. This business sold within the first 30 days for the full asking price. One key factor to the successful sale was the seller understanding that he needed to stay on for an extended amount of time in order to ensure the least amount of attrition for the buyers. To my knowledge, not a single account was lost due to the transfer.

Chapter One

DECIDING TO SELL OR NOT

THERE ARE THREE FACTORS IN DECIDING TO SELL OR NOT. FIRST IS THE timing in your life, second is the market's timing, and third is the businesses life. I say businesses life because a business is alive, it's a living breathing thing that is as fragile as anything else that is alive. Whether you're personally ready or not is a big decision to make but it doesn't have to be the end of your working career. Many of my sellers went on to open or purchase completely different businesses, which can be very reassuring to those who are afraid to let go. The interesting thing is that when you are so busy running the business you own, you don't see or expose yourself to new opportunities. Once you have decided to sell, suddenly new ideas and new situations just present themselves, and you start picturing yourself doing something new. Selling your business is a process that you must allow to unfold as time moves forward.

Many of the sellers who call me are burnt out and tired of their business, but they are still reluctant to let it go. I tell them that unless they are ready to truly breathe new life into the current or next year then life will not be any different than it already is. If you hang on to something that you really don't want to do then it will most likely go down, not up. Interestingly, I have never met a seller who didn't have a whole slew of ideas on how to improve the business. Of course, the question to ask is, "*Why haven't you already done all these wonderful things?*" The truth is, anyone who has run their own business understands that you hit a wall at some point, and rather than go to the next stage, they just get comfortable where they are.

1

They know what they should do but they just don't want to do it. This is the junction that many sellers face, continue working on improving it or sell it. Ideally, if you want to work on improving it the time to start is a couple of years before putting it on the market. If you don't have a few years or even a few months don't fret about it! It's ok that you didn't do everything to make the business perfect. Most buyers have hope that your business can do more, so your helpful ideas are going to motivate the next person running the business.

If you are considering the best time to retire from working, I suggest that just as you had a business plan, you'll need a retirement plan. Retirement is unique to each individual, but it is whatever you want it to be. There is no rule that says once you hit a certain age that you must be put out to pasture. There is a common-sense rule, though, that says you shouldn't let emotion make you hold on when you should be letting go. And don't be the guy who says he would sell it for the right price because, that's usually a self-saboteur who sets up impossible road blocks because they don't really want to sell. If you really want to sell it, then be practical, and listen to the expert, who knows about the real value of similar businesses that have sold. Don't be afraid of selling your business. If you are the type of person who was strong enough to build a successful business, then you can certainly do many productive and relevant things with your retirement. The trick is to get out while the business is strong and healthy—and so are you!

The timing of the market is the second element of selling. The first business broker I ever worked for said that he got into selling businesses because it was recession proof. "When the market is strong we do well, when the market takes a hit, we have a whole new segment of buyers who have been displaced from their employment." That was true, except for the great recession of 2008, when we saw every industry fall off the edge. We had no access to capital because banks were not lending, and personal portfolios were rapidly descending into the abyss. What you might not realize is that we, the M&A Business Brokers, had difficulty selling anything for several years after. Most buyers want to see three years of good financials, as do the banks. That recession was so widespread that for years after, it was very difficult to sell anything that wasn't a fire sale. That is not the way anyone wants to exit their business.

In order for the timing to be right in the market, there must be confidence in the market in general, and access to inexpensive capital or low interest rates. And there is another factor that business owners must be more aware of: obsolescence, the third of timing the sale.

When I first began my M&A career it was so difficult to sell a "*virtual*" business. Buyers wanted to drive up to a place and touch a door handle for their money, but now things have changed. Buyers are much savvier and understanding about cash flow and liability. A business today is not judged solely on cash flow but more on its overall manageability. Players like Amazon have been game changers, they have redefined the way that consumers shop and the way that the retail supply chain manages products. If you own a business that has been declining over the years, you must find another way to evolve or your business will either sell for very little or not at all. I receive too many calls from buyers who are stuck in the past, telling me how great their businesses were years ago. My answer is always the same, "*Well then you should have sold it years ago when it was making more money.*"

The timing of selling your business is an art. If you wait too long you risk obsolescence, or your waning interest will erode the constant upgrading and innovation the business needs in order to stay competitive. The very best time to sell is the hardest time to sell, when the business is doing its very best. It finally has a good solid management team in place and the sales are thriving—that is the right time to sell. This is when you'll get top dollar for it, and when you'll have the most interest from buyers.

It's your business and you have options, so let's look at your options with frankness. You could keep working in the business until one of you dies—not the best option, unless you don't care about your time left in the world, or the longevity of the business you created. I have sold many businesses in my life, and I will tell you that every seller I ever dealt with cared to some degree about the business carrying on without them. They love the fact that something they were part of building will outlive them, and that it is part of their legacy.

Another option is to pass the business on to your child or your heir. Well here is a sad statistic: 70% of wealthy families lose their wealth by the second generation. Relationships are complicated, and that would need a separate book. I will only say that it is a very special kind of family that has groomed an heir to take over all aspects of the business, and it's an extra special business owner who has timed his/her exit so that both the business and the heir can succeed.

The bottom line is that you want to be in the driver's seat when selling. The worst calls I get are from clients who are sick, and desperately looking for a buyer. Desperation is never good, and having time on your side allows for a better deal to transpire. So, with that said, now you may be asking, *"What do I have to do to sell my business?"* Please read on...

KEEP
CALM

AND
AND GET

PREPARED

WITH C.B.B.

Chapter Two

PREPARATION AND VALUING

"*BE PREPARED*" IS NOT JUST THE MOTTO OF THE BOY SCOUTS, IT'S ALSO THE motto for selling a business. I have been a busy business owner myself for many years, I cannot condone poor bookkeeping just because you have a lot going on. It is impossible to sell a business for top dollar if you don't really have a handle on the books. The time to be concerned about it is NOW if you plan on selling within three years, otherwise you are seriously limiting your chances of a successful sale, just because you didn't hire a bookkeeper to organize the business. Not only will buyers expect it, but as a business owner, if you don't have that top-down view of what's going on in your own business, it's hard to see what needs to be done in order to improve it. So, even if you are only doing it for a potential sale, I am sure you will see some value in spending the money required to have it done correctly. Otherwise, it's like driving your car with a blindfold on, and that's just not a good idea.

Pre-sale planning begins with defining your goals and objectives. These include both your personal and business goals. The process of selling a business has become more complex today. Buyers are more cautious and much more rigorous in their due diligence efforts due to the recession. A big reason why deals fail is that owners do not plan early enough to sell their business. Proper planning can allow for corporate restructuring if necessary, and this could save thousands of dollars in post-sale gains. Many first-time sellers fail to realize that it takes time and careful planning to optimize the business's value which in turn will maximize the sale price. So, if you're planning on selling within the next three years, start assembling your team now, and get to work, planning to get the best out of what you've built.

WHAT DO MOST BUYERS WANT?

*Clean books and records
*Reoccurring revenue
*SBA qualified (up to 5 million)
*Niche businesses
*Service businesses
*B to B businesses
*Uncomplicated businesses to learn
*Slow and steady growth
*Three years of consistent profit
*Minimal number of employees
*Transferable contracts
*No client concentration
*Equipment in very good condition
*Supportive seller who cares post sale

Knowing what buyers are looking for is a good place to start with your preparation to sell the business. If your business doesn't fall into all the categories above, then ask yourself if there is anything that you could do presale to improve some of these things. This might be a good time to consult with a value coach to help you hone in on some specific things that you could focus on to make the business as desirable as possible. There is a buyer for almost every business but it's a game of odds, and the odds favor you if you have a business that appeals to the greatest number of potential buyers.

The most helpful tool I give sellers is the view from the other seat. Sometimes when they are talking about their business I repeat back what they've said, but from the buyer's point of view. This allows sellers to take another perspective of their business, to see how an outside source might value what they've built. It sounds obvious, but I assure you that it happens all the time. That leads us on to another important subject: "*What is my business worth?"* The answer is simply, "whatever someone is willing to pay."

Desirability changes as time goes on and you must be aware of that. Businesses have seasons of popularity, and that highly affects the buyer pool for your type of industry. One of the key elements in selling your business is the timing of your industry in the market. The saddest thing I see is people hanging on for too long and then regretting it afterwards. A buyer will pay more for a business that he/or she perceives is currently popular due to the buzz they are hearing about a particular industry.

Remember what Dale Carnegie said? *"Class, do you know what ASSUME means? Don't Make an Ass Out of You and Me!"* The point is not to assume what the business is worth without having it professionally valued by a business broker or M&A transaction specialist. They will give you an opinion of value using both their skill and experience. This part is very important. Would you go to your doctor and ask him to fix your car? No. How about finding out that you need brain surgery but insisting your podiatrist do it? Sounds crazy, right? So why do business owners ask their accountant or an attorney to value their business? I know the answer is because the business owners trust them. You should trust them, but for their respective skills and accreditations, not for things outside their experience and expertise. Many accountants and attorneys have referred business owners to me, but there are some who might see an opportunity for business for themselves. The best analogy I can give is jewelry appraisal. If I take a piece of jewelry to my jeweler and ask her for an appraisal, she'll give an official appraisal, and for insurance purposes, that is perfect. Now, if I want to sell that piece of jewelry and I take it to a pawnbroker, will I get the same price as the appraisal? No, obviously not. Anyone who has ever hosted a garage sale knows that what you paid for an item, or what you think it's worth is hardly relevant. If you really want to know the value of what something will sell for, you should ask the person who sells that item for a living, not someone who deals in the theory of value—unless theory is what you're looking for.

Sellers have all kinds of misconceptions about their business's value—both too high and too low. Believe it or not there is a real science to valuing businesses, and a professional, like myself, must have many certifications and training to be able to properly evaluate it. That, coupled with real street experience, can give a seller a range or an opinion of value. I am a big believer in getting into the market at the right price. Sometimes sellers insist on listing it at the very top end of the scale, and then when it doesn't sell we have to reduce the price. I don't want to leave any money on the table for sellers, but it also doesn't look good when a listing sits around for a long time without selling, and then the price drops. On the other hand, I've had a few instances when I changed the price to the highest end of the spectrum due to the popularity, interest and surplus of available buyers. In summary, valuing a business is part science and part voodoo. I get a feeling about where the price should be in order to get it sold, based on the market rhythm—and the market always tells us everything. All a good broker can do is represent it accurately, and fully understand the complexities of both the business and its financials as it pertains to the buyer. A good broker with significant experience should be able to give you the right advice for your specific business and area.

VALUE

If valuing a business was as easy as EBITDA (earnings before interest, taxes, depreciation, and amortization) multiplied by five, or SDE (seller's discretionary earnings) times 2.5, then I might as well ask for my money back on the two degrees I have in valuing businesses. I am hoping my sarcasm resonates with you! People call me and ask me to spit out this confirmation all the time—I think they want an idea of what it would sell for, but are afraid to go down that path. So I say, first things first. Decide when you want to sell and then start planning for it. I am more than happy to start working with a client well in advance of their intended selling time. However, remember that the value could change completely by the time you decide to list it, due to market conditions. Below is a story about a deal that I closed in 2017. Several years ago, I had a lot of trouble selling e-commerce businesses. People weren't sure if they would last or grow, and they weren't sure that they had enough knowledge of the back end to run it. Now we know it's the star of the show. Maybe in 10 years it won't be desirable anymore, but who knows? Timing and value go hand in hand.

Case Study 2.

Last year I sold a $6M supplement company. When I first took the listing, it was tricky to value because they had solid evidence of their tremendous growth, but prior years' financials didn't support that price tag. As I mentioned before, sometimes it's not strictly about cash flow if the business type is very desirable. So I had to find a strategic buyer who might have a business that was also in their wheelhouse and could find intrinsic value—and I did. The buyers were also in the supplement business, but their primary sales channel was through the medical profession. My seller's primary sales channel was through Amazon and their own website. This was a marriage made in heaven, because in addition to the ever-increasing cash flow that was increasing literally every month, their model could help their current business become easier to operate and more profitable. This company also had the new phenomenon of doing a tremendous amount of business without any need of employees, rent, or equipment. This company was virtual, which means they never touched the product—not when it was made, not when it shipped to fulfillment, and not when it shipped to the customer. I sold a $6M business and the buyer gained two laptops plus a way to double its current business. That is a strategic buyer.

Now you might be wondering why they wanted to sell this awesome business. They were two guys that were friends in high school, and had partnered from the beginning of the business. They had differing skill sets that helped the business grow to its current level, but they had one huge problem: they simply couldn't stand each other anymore. They were constantly fighting about every aspect of the business, and after my first phone meeting with them, I too realized that if they didn't sell, eventually it would implode, considering the degree of animosity emanating from both sides. I truly felt like a marriage counselor throughout the time I worked with them. My goal was to be the peace-keeper so we could get this deal done. We structured the sale with both the owners retaining a small part of the business and staying involved, but having little contact with each other. Following up post sale, I'm happy to report that everyone is staying in their corners (boxing analogy) and the business is thriving. Sometimes separation from your partner can be healthy.

Case Study 3.

I went on a listing call once for a home care facility. This type of business sends people to older folks' homes to help them get around, take their medications, give them company, do some errands for them, etc. The business provided me with the current year financials (about eight months of the year,) I gave them a price and we listed the business. Right afterwards, I asked them for all the remaining financials consisting of three years of tax returns, financial statements and balance sheets. Once I had reviewed all these documents, I discovered that the cash flow was even higher than I first thought, based on incomplete information. So I increased the listing price, which isn't just about the cash flow, it's also about desirability, and that's the voodoo part. It's hard to quantify desirability unless you have a lot of experience, and your broker understands the market. Some businesses have fads, just like bell bottom jeans and parachute pants. This listing landed right at the time of the home healthcare business fad. This type of business gained a lot of popularity because of all the aging baby boomer articles. Suddenly, it became a great investment idea, and everybody wanted to buy one or start one. If you feel like there is a lot of positive buzz about your type of business, then the timing might be ideal to find a buyer. That business got a full price offer in the first month.

Chapter 3

EXIT AND LISTING TEAM

CHOOSING THE RIGHT TEAM TO HELP YOU EXIT YOUR BUSINESS IS YOUR next important step. To fortify the processes laid out in the previous chapter, in preparation for going to market you must assemble your team. Your team should include a bookkeeper, an accountant or CPA, a business attorney, and a business broker, or mergers and acquisition specialist. You may need an escrow company, but your broker should work with more than one. Everyone on the team has a role to play and they must interact well with each other. Please pay attention to the following: *You are the client and the head of the team. We work for you, not the other way around.* There is a fine balance between clients that think they know everything and clients that let the "professionals" run amuck. Neither are good, so exercise common sense and all will be fine. I am referring to spending $1,000 in order to save $100. It's easy to get carried away with the minutia of a deal, but that can easily end up costing a small fortune. Stay focused on the important aspects. You've managed to run your own business so far and you can do this too.

You don't know what you don't know. The wisest people I know admit to how little they know. The reason you need a team behind you isn't to create billable hours of expense, but to provide you with invaluable knowledge on structuring the business and thus the sale, in the most advantageous way for you—the client. If the people on your team can't do that, then you need a new roster.

The structure of your company can have a huge impact on the post-sale tax consequence. Working with CPAs, tax attorneys, and financial advisors can significantly help you to keep as much money as possible after the sale. However, these changes often must be done prior to finding a buyer. This is all part of the preparation plan. Your CPA should be advising you about your choices of C-corporation, S-corporation or some pass-through entity, and how this will affect your pre and post-sale money. This book is written from a business broker's perspective, so the advice given is from that perspective. Just as I ask other professionals to stay in their area of expertise, so will I. I can only advise that some planning advisors can be of great help to sellers, but just because you have known your accountant for a long time and you trust them to do your taxes, that doesn't mean he/she is the most qualified person to advise you about selling the business and keeping the most money in your pocket. Ask questions and discover all the options available for your situation and business. While I don't endorse corporate restructure unless necessary, there are many reasons to explore all your options in order to reduce your tax burden post sale. For example, C-corporations are subject to double taxation.

DEFERRED SALE TRUSTS

One option to alleviate post sale tax is a deferred sales trust and very often this is something your accountant might not even be aware of. There are many companies that specialize in this type of trust. It is important to speak with the most reputable of companies if you are interested in this type of program. The caveat is that companies that provide this service have an advisory role and they are going to manage the money, so you need to weigh the risk.

The sale of a business is not usually a sale of only one asset. Instead, all the assets of the business are sold. Generally, each asset is treated as being sold separately, for the purposes of determining a gain or loss.

A business usually has many assets. When sold, they must be classified as capital assets, depreciable property used in the business, real property used in the business, or property held for sale to customers, such as inventory or stock in trade. The gain or loss on each asset is calculated separately. The sale of capital assets results in capital gain or loss. The sale of real property or depreciable property used in the business and held longer than one year will result in a gain or loss from a section 1231 transaction. The sale of inventory results in ordinary income or loss.

Goodwill in a business sale is treated as a long-term capital gain and therefore carries favorable tax treatment at the time the payments are actually received. In this analysis, where each class of assets is potentially taxed at a separate rate, ordinary income versus capital gains, in the construct of the DST (deferred sales trust), the client's payments from the DST usually consist initially of interest payments on the note. Often people take income only and choose to perpetually defer the capital gains taxes. For others, the income they receive from the DST is taxed at ordinary income tax rates. As the seller receives distributions of principal, the distributions will be reported for them at the end of the year, detailing the amount of the principal payments that represent long term capital gains, the amount generated from depreciation recapture, and the amount deemed as ordinary income. The tax rates for the distributions are then applied proportionally against the total principal received for a given year. DSTs are a good option for sellers who are not in immediate need of all the proceeds.

BROKERS

When considering a broker to represent you, choose carefully. They will be representing you and your company's integrity. It would be a shame to have your legacy marred because of someone who is supposed to shine the best light possible on you but doesn't. I like to work with clients who hold a shared set of values and integrity and I recommend that you do the same. The truth is always the best story anyone ever told or heard. You don't have to worry about anything bad surfacing later on, and buyers truly buy businesses so that they can improve them, not because they are already perfect. So don't worry about the warts of the business —or indeed of the owner. To find the right buyer, you must present the whole story, just as it is. The key is to let the broker know about every possible negative element from the beginning. Just about the worst thing that can happen in a due diligence meeting is to have the buyer spring something out of the blue that your broker didn't know about. It happens very rarely to me because I warn my sellers not to do that, but it has happened. It almost always kills the deal, looking like a deliberate attempt to hide something.

In the State of California, business brokers are governed by the Department of Real Estate. M&A advisors who do larger deals might also have a securities license and a Broker Dealer. Since I rarely handle real estate, but always deal with business transactions, there are two major associations that are relevant to the credibility of a business broker: the California Association of Business Brokers, and the International Association of Business Brokers. Both associations have certification programs, and anyone who is serious about their profession should make the time and expense to become certified. Mergers and Acquisitions have the M&A Source.

Continued education is important because there is only a handful of serious professional business brokers & M&A specialists compared to real estate salespeople and brokers. Many individual business brokers are isolated, and lack the experience to get through a transaction unscathed if they don't have a support system behind them. I have been in this profession for 14 years and I still come across something new every now and then. Remember, you don't know what you don't know.

Business brokers can, and do, represent both sides of the transaction over 90% of the time, and if they don't have adequate experience, that could be a serious problem. Both the buyer and the seller are counting on a broker's knowledge to facilitate a smooth transaction, and to avoid positioning them in harm's way. A lack of experience and knowledge can be dangerous to all parties from both a liability and fiduciary perspective.

MAYBE I'LL JUST SELL IT MYSELF

There's a famous quote regarding having a fool for a lawyer if representing yourself and it applies here as well. I know you are thinking that I'm biased, because I'm the broker and I profit from the sale. Well yes, that's how I make my crazy living. However, remember this: you don't know what you don't know? Business brokers charge a significant commission because it is not easy to sell a business, it's not black and white, as it is with real estate, and it's also very emotional. It is certainly not a sure thing. I have worked a year or longer on a listing just to have it not sell. Think about that. A year of talking, answering the phone, driving to appointments, and creating loads of paperwork—all for nothing! It's hard work making a living as a business broker. When I was an agent working for my first broker, he said the failure rate for people trying to be a business broker was 90%. That's staggering, right? I repeat, it is not easy to successfully and competently sell businesses.

WHAT COULD GO WRONG?

Everything will fall apart five times before it closes—if it closes. The biggest mistake sellers make in hiring a broker, or not hiring a broker, is to think the only thing they do is find a buyer. I wish that was the only thing I had to do. My job is like one of those escape room venues, the ones where you pay someone to stick you in a room with no visible escape and you must think your way out. My job is like that, because when the whole deal comes crashing down because of some unforeseen cataclysmic event, I must think of a way, a new vantage point, in order to overcome the problem and get the deal done. I compare my work with buyers to "herding cats in a rain storm with thunder and lightning." Here's a short list of <u>some</u> of the things that I've had to deal with so far in my career:

- Relationship problems between partners
- Relationship problems between seller and spouse
- Crazy things coming up on UCC1 searches
- Death
- Lies—ALL kinds of lies!
- Audit—ALL agencies (local tax, federal tax, EDD, workers' comp, criminal, FBI, local law enforcement, and more)
- Employees quitting
- Top account lost during the sale
- Old people and young people
- Drunk or high people (both sellers and buyers)

Case Study 4.

I have done well over 300 lease assignments and they are not all the same. A case in point: I once had a seller who praised my knowledge of lease assignments because he was involved in a nightmare from a previous sale of a food wholesale business he used to own.

He shared his story about selling the business many years before when he carried a note on the sale. The problem was the way the lease assignment had been handled by the broker, and the amount of the note as a percentage of the total sale. In this case, the buyer was not an honest person. He was looking for someone who would take a big note on the business, and then never made a single payment on the note. Most notes have the business as collateral, which is fine if you can still get into the business. Unfortunately, the broker was ignorant to the fact that industrial leases almost always fully assign without keeping the seller on as a guarantor, thus not allowing the seller to get back into the business in a worst-case scenario, and that is exactly what happened. The buyer changed the locks on the doors, and when the seller showed up with the police, they said he had no right to enter because he wasn't on the lease. The seller could not collect his collateral without significant legal expense. In the end, the stress affected him so adversely he decided to let it go and refocus on building something new rather than risking becoming financially drained from legal fees and suffering a nervous breakdown. I like to finish my stories on a positive note, so I will disclose that we did sell his new business for top dollar and he made a great profit on the sale with no issues!

Case Study 5.

I once had a listing for a Dairy Queen franchise. The seller had purchased the business for his wife, who really didn't want to work there. Never buy a business for a spouse unless it's truly something they desire to do and not something you want them to do because you think it will be good for them. After a few months she got bored with the business and didn't want to operate it anymore. So the husband brought his brother-in-law in to run it—until he found another job. Then the husband brought his sister-in-law to work there, but she would bring along her new baby and perch him on the front counter— and she barely spoke English. I promise I'm not making this up!

One day, a buyer called and said, "tell me about this Dairy Queen." I told him all the above, including the latest news, that the seller had put a karaoke machine in the entrance. The prospective buyer laughed and went for a visit. Three hours later, he called to tell me about his visit. First, he saw the karaoke machine and shook his head. Then he discretely pretended to look at birthday cakes and he told the employee, whose baby was sitting on the counter crying, that he was considering buying a birthday cake for his son. She responded with "Oh no, you should buy cake from Baskin Robbins it better than this one (sic)." The buyer told me to write up an offer immediately because he felt that no one could do worse than these people!

Sometimes sellers feel that everything must be perfect in the business, but that's not the case at all. Buyers are looking for potential, with a dream of improving the business with whatever skills they bring to the deal. They want to build on what you've done so far; they want to take it to the next level.

Chapter 4

KISSING FROGS

WHO WILL BUY MY BUSINESS?

SELLERS OF SMALL BUSINESSES OFTEN THINK THAT A COMPETITOR WOULD be the most ideal buyer for their business. I think they get this idea from the news when they hear of M&A deals for top dollar. It is very true in M&A, but it rarely happens in small business. In smaller deals, typically under 2 or 3 million, the purchaser will most likely be an individual, or a private buyer, because they pay better than competitors. They could be someone from a related industry that has become displaced from their regular employment and is ready to break out on their own. If the buyer doesn't have direct experience in the field of the business they will often be ok with paying a higher multiplier in order to learn. I attribute the increase in purchase price as the barrier-to-enter fee, it's all part of the goodwill. These types of buyers need the structure and the experience of the seller to guide them in running this type of business, and for that, they are usually willing to pay a bit more. Direct competitors are not in need of your industry teachings, but they are interested in your suppliers, customers, and sometimes employees. Often an individual is a great buyer because he will probably obtain an SBA loan to purchase the business, thus freeing up cash for operating expenses, and not requiring you to finance the entire sale. That doesn't mean you won't be asked to finance some of the transaction. Many buyers and banks believe that the seller should have skin in the game and share the risk. However, the percentage can be very fair, as low as 10% of the purchase price. There are several advantages of doing this; one is that it shows the buyers that you have confidence in the business you're selling. It can also make the buyer feel more comfortable that you are willing to stay in touch with them should they need any of your guidance or help in the future. Another clear advantage to you is that you will offset the income received into multiple tax years, and this deferral can be very helpful, depending on the income received in these years from other sources, and the available write-offs during that time. One downside of an SBA loan is that the seller's note is going to be in the second position of priority. This means that in a case of bankruptcy, you will come in behind the bank. If it's not an SBA loan and is just a seller note, then you have the collateral of the business, unless otherwise specified, and in a worst-case scenario you could take back the business. In cases where you've financed under 25% of the sale, it's considered a low risk because you're collecting on the note monthly in most cases, and if the note isn't too long, or isn't too high a percentage of the total acquisition, you have a good chance of collecting it all.

This is worth repeating; a common misconception with sellers is that they think the most important thing I do is produce a buyer. While technically, according to real estate law, that is exactly what I need to do to earn my commission, that isn't what I'm talking about. Finding a buyer isn't that difficult. Finding the right buyer AND getting all the way to a close is a totally different ball game. The first broker I ever worked for (yes him again—the treasure trove of wisdom!) told me, "Christina, every deal you do will fall apart approximately five times before it closes. How you deal with all the problems that arise will determine whether you can do this for a living or not." Fourteen years later that is still the best advice I have received, and a mantra I repeat in my head often when it's all falling apart around me. Real estate home sales are repetitive stuff. Business brokers deal with so many third-party issues, there are so many potential pitfalls, it's almost impossible to be completely prepared for what you'll have to face. Remember, the business is alive: sometimes it has a landlord, and it has various agencies to deal with like EDD, ABC, postings, tax liens, employees, partners, etc., and at every turn something can go wrong. Your team should get you through these potential minefields and that is how businesses are sold successfully. I have been doing this for over 14 years and I still find myself saying every now and then, *"Wow, I've never seen that happen before!"* I have had people die during a deal. I've had dead people show up on a UCC search filing (that's no fun BTW). I've dealt with divorcing and divorced sellers. I've had businesses shut down during escrow, screaming matches in partnership disputes, audits from the Employment Development Department, Federal, and State Tax agencies, health department problems, liquor license problems up to the wazoo; I have seen corrupt landlords, oblivious landlords and, sometimes, a pleasant and decent landlord.

The title of this chapter is called kissing frogs because just like a princess, you might need to kiss a few frogs before you find Prince Charming. Because I've done so many business sales and maybe because I have great intuition too, I know when I've found the right buyer. It's like a key in a lock, everything just fits into place.

A bunch of things will go wrong at some point, and if you don't have the right buyer, they will probably bail out. It's scary buying a business. There are many unknowns to the buyer and they're working on the good faith that your business is as great as you've told them it is, and that they can run it at least as well as you do. They must be brave, and there must be synergy between all the parties. Often, I feel like more of a counselor than a broker, trying to get both parties to empathize with each other, and that is another difference between selling homes and selling businesses. A very successful real estate agent friend of mine told me that she tries at all costs to get the seller out of the house so that the buyer never meets them. In my case it's just the opposite: they must not only meet, but they must also like each other, so that some form of trust can be established. The business is alive, and if you buy a business from a shady guy you are likely to have shady dealings within the business.

Another thing you can do in preparation to sell is to put a solid management team in place. It's much easier to sell a business that can run independently. If possible, wean yourself out of the critical day-to-day operations as early as possible prior to selling, as this will give your business the highest desirability. The buyer's concern will always be the continued success of the business after the sale, so retaining key employees is crucial to the continuity of the business once it's sold. In addition, cross training employees in smaller businesses is wise, in case there is some attrition after the sale, so at least other employees can fill in until the position can be filled again. Many things can come up in a listing. The key is to have an experienced team behind you that is ready to handle any given situation.

Case Study 6.

As I have said in prior chapters, I pride myself on having a matchmaker-like ability to pair up buyers and sellers. I have a sixth sense which lets me know if I've found the right person to buy the business, and I've been right every time except once. I once had a seller of a soda distribution business and they had an exclusive formula of sodas that tasted similar to the original flavors. They sold these sodas to restaurants, bars and convenience stores. One day, a yuppie 30-something couple contacted me to visit the business. As soon as I saw them and spoke to them I told the seller not to get his hopes up, they weren't right for the business. Surprisingly, they made an offer which was close to full price. They had the money and credit, so the seller agreed but I wasn't convinced, because I just couldn't see them in that type of business. They went to escrow to sign their documents and I got a call from the escrow officer saying that my clients behaved oddly when they were there. I asked in what way, she said they were fondling all over each other in the office, it wasn't appropriate and it was bizarre. I wasn't sure what to think about that, other than the reinforcing thought that they weren't a good fit. The whole 30 days the escrow went on I was convinced they would pull out, but they didn't, and the deal closed. When the seller did his training they also acted weird with him, and he mentioned that the wife was very controlling. About six months later I received a call from the buyer saying he was having trouble running the business because his wife wouldn't let him visit the bars, even during the day! I encouraged counseling, and if that didn't work, then he would either have to hire sales staff or sell the business. A year after he had bought it he called to say that they had divorced and he wanted to sell it. Still today after all the deals I have done, that one was very odd. I guess I was right after all!

Case Study 7.

When I take a listing, I try to answer all the seller's questions to the best of my knowledge. I took on an owner-operated, one-person business years ago when I was still relatively new to brokering—a franchise that offered in-home services, selling and installing window blinds. It was profitable and had clean books, but I told the seller that these kinds of businesses are difficult to sell, and that he would have to be patient. He said that was fine with him, if it took a year then it took a year, he wasn't in a rush.

Usually, I find my buyers when they call or email in for a business listing. One time though, a gentleman had called me about a certain business, but the owner had just accepted an offer, so I had to decline his interest. A few weeks later he emailed me on another that was also in escrow. A month later, he called me on another listing, I felt terrible telling him that I had just received another offer on it! He said, "You must be the busiest business broker in Orange County!" I told him to tell me what kind of business he was looking for because his choices were all over the map. He said that he liked working in a hands-on type of business, saying that he was a handy people person, and he would have to involve his son in the business. I told him to hear me out, I had this blind business I wanted to present to him. Long story short: I set up a call between them that night. It went so well they set up a ride-along meeting the next day. The buyer made a full price offer and the seller was thrilled, the deal closed about a month later. When I followed up after, the buyer said, "In a million years I would have never looked into that kind of business, but I love it!"

Case Study 8.

I received a phone call from a landlord that had a tenant who was eight months behind on their rent, and the rent was over $7,000 a month. He went on to explain that the tenant had been there 18 years and had been good until after the recession. Then she *had been either late with rent or did not make payments at all. By the time he contacted me she was $62,000 in arrears. I told him I would speak to her and do my best to help.*

There is a small segment of businesses that can be sold even if they aren't profitable, and it's mainly restaurants. If the location is good, it has a solid build-out, a willing landlord and a liquor license then it can often be sold as an asset sale. The term, "asset sale" is confusing because most of the transactions I do are asset sales. There are two types of potential sales: stock sales and asset sales. Stock sales have both benefits and risks. However, if it isn't necessary, then most buyers prefer an asset sale as it has far less liability for them. When a business transfers as an asset sale, then there's a clear cut from the old and the new owner, this process is a bulk sale and subject to the bulk sale law. Usually we allow a special bulk sale escrow to complete the transfer (more about that later).

I went to see the delinquent tenant and she was as hostile as they get. The only reason she made the appointment was because the landlord had threatened her. After spending an hour with her and getting her to open up to me, I found out that this restaurant was her whole life. She was terrified at the thought of not having it anymore. Further than that, she had begged, borrowed, and practically stolen from everyone around her. She befriended a wealthy Japanese woman and managed to get over $250,000 from her with no way of paying it back. She herself was Japanese, and this was a source of humiliation for her, but her need to keep the business going at any cost pushed her forward. By the time she finished her confessions to me I realized that the debts were much greater than I could sell it for, but she did have a great location, a liquor license, a willing landlord to get something rather than nothing, and the seller herself saw the possibility of not declaring bankruptcy, which would allow her to save face.

I found a buyer almost immediately and disclosed the situation. Luckily, they were patient and understanding. I sold the business for $175,000, not nearly enough to cover the debts *that I knew about (let alone those I didn't) but it was a fair price for a business that wasn't making any money.*

Once we opened escrow it seemed there were more debtors coming out of the woodwork, a total of $550,000 in fact. We'll it wasn't easy, but I negotiated with all of them so that everyone would get something, because the alternative was that she would go bankrupt and no one would get anything. To this day, I've never taken on such a crazy deal, nor do I want to ever again, but I'm happy that everyone got something. The seller was able to save face with a friend, and culturally I knew how important that was to her.

Chapter 5

THE OFFER

The offer is a big deal, it's the beginning of the end game— getting it sold! While I wouldn't rely on spit and a handshake, offers are promises to do something if everything else checks out. Offers can come in two forms: an LOI (letter of intent), or as a purchase agreement. In smaller deals, I prefer to go right to a purchase agreement but in larger deals its best to start with an LOI because the terms will probably be drawn up with an attorney. Let's start with an LOI.

A letter of intent is exactly that. It states the general intentions of the buyer and is purposely vague and ambiguous. It's used because there are many unknowns of the business at its early stages and the buyer doesn't want to commit to more until they are given more information. If you are buying a large business with many employees, contracts, suppliers and other entities, then you might want to reserve the ability to redraw what you want for a later date, rather than lay it all out upfront. Most LOIs contain the basics, such as the buyer's details, the purchase price and the general terms. It's a feeler to see if there's a synergy at all between buyer and seller that can be utilized to put a deal together. Most LOI's are non-binding for either party so they can be canceled at any point, unless a binding provision is inserted. Due diligence is rigorous, and if a deal is going to die, it might be at that stage, but it can also be due to the terms. For instance, an LOI can say that a certain amount will be on a seller note but the length will be negotiated later. You assume that it will be reasonable, but when the attorney sends over the first draft you realize you're on different planets, and the middle ground is far away. That's why the more important points should be laid out in the beginning, so that no-one's time and money is wasted.

If an attorney is writing up the purchase agreement, the seller will need their own attorney, and so will the buyer, so that both sides can be represented fairly. If you don't have a competent business attorney on speed dial, don't worry. Your broker should be able to refer you to one. Be prepared, as there is a lot of negotiation back and forth, and the legal fees can be significant if it's a large and complex business. However, it's money well spent, because often these documents govern your involvement in the future and monetary disbursement. All subsequent documents to the purchase agreement are either addendums or exhibits, and they can include employment agreements, disclosures, contribution agreements, specific non-competes, corporate structures and more.

In California, if you buy a house, the form used to write up the offer will be from the California Bureau of Real Estate (BRE), and it will have all the necessary disclosures according to real estate law. In business brokering, we could use a form provided by BRE, but I personally prefer the CABB (California Association of Business Brokers) forms, because they are simple and written in plain English, so you can understand the language without the services of an interpreter. The forms have been through the legal system countless times, they have a more predictable outcome than a custom purchase agreement written up by an attorney. For smaller businesses, it is usually unnecessary to spend money on custom forms unless there are special circumstances. In the purchase agreement, you should have the exact terms of the purchase price, the amount of the deposit, when and how the balance will be funded, the buyer's identity (corporation or individual), the expectations for training, a non-compete clause, the assets that will be transferred, details of the individual who will pay for the lease assignment, the details of both parties' brokers, duration of the offer's validity, duration of the due diligence period, and any other detail that needs to be addressed.

An issue that regularly arises is the length of time the seller needs to stay in the business post-sale. There is no set answer, and it's really a common-sense problem. If you have problems delegating, and you have either taken on all the important roles, or you constantly undermine the employees by stepping in, then be prepared for a long exit. The point I am trying to make is that you really need to build up a business to be sold by empowering the employees to take responsibility for their roles. If you feel that you could go on vacation for three weeks and everything would operate just fine without you, then you've done well, and it will be easier to sell your business.

Once a buyer has presented you with an offer, you may accept it, counter the offer, or let it expire. I don't recommend the third option. Each broker has their own style, and I can only explain my own procedure, which has been successful for me. I don't feel comfortable pushing a deal into escrow unless I'm confident it's going to close. Therefore, once an offer has been agreed by both parties there is a due diligence period, and its duration should have been specified in the purchase agreement. The seller is bound to work with the buyer to complete the due diligence period, and if the buyer doesn't wish to move forward after they have been through due diligence, then the seller can accept another offer, or a backup offer will be in the first position. Selling a business is stressful enough for everyone; there is no reason to incur escrow expenses if the deal is going to fall apart. I tell my sellers that if we make it through escrow then they have a solid chance of closing the deal. I will say, though, that it isn't a done deal until it closes, and many problems can arise during this time. Don't stop running the business as though you own it, and don't reduce the hours of the business because you're already on marguerita time.

Case Study 9.

Many people ask me how these businesses fare after the sale. Usually they continue to do well—in some cases better than before. I did have a bizarre transaction once though. I had a very successful Italian restaurant and bar with entertainment listing. A great business with a terrific vibe. The business had a solid reputation and had been operating without any significant issues for several years. A buyer contacted me to go and see the business, and during the tour he commented how much he liked the place. The next night he visited for dinner and the next day he called to say that it was just great, and he would like to make an offer. The offer was accepted, and we went through due diligence and then escrow. Escrow is longer when you're transferring a liquor license, and during that time he and the seller spoke off and on. The buyer told him how perfect the business was for him and how he wouldn't change a thing. So far it sounds logical and normal, right? We closed escrow, and as is customary, the seller met the buyer at the restaurant the next day to show him how to open, and how to operate everything, but he didn't seem to be paying much attention. The seller called me to say the buyer had acted quite strange and told him not to come back the next day, he would call him if he had any questions. My seller was curious, so he drove to the restaurant the next day and saw a big sign saying "Closed for renovations." Then the employees started calling, saying that the new owner had told them not to come in until they were called back. One week later the business reopened as a BBQ restaurant with a new chef, décor, name and—to my knowledge—without the permission of the landlord. Now it's true that once someone buys a business it's theirs to do with as they wish, but why in the world would you pay top dollar for a concept that is functioning well in order to change it into something entirely different? I will never get the answer to that question, not one that makes sense anyway. It was the fastest bankruptcy from a business acquisition I had ever seen. In just three months, they closed their doors permanently. Strange, indeed!

Chapter 6

DUE DILIGENCE

THE DUE DILIGENCE PROCESS IS SIMPLY A BUYER WANTING TO TAKE A closer look at the business. If you've prepared properly, then there shouldn't be any big surprises. But there usually are some. The more you dig into something, the greater the chance of uncovering something either beneficial or detrimental to you. One thing I've learned is that if a deal is meant to work out, it will. The more you have to convince someone that this is the right deal for them, the more likely that they are not the right buyer for you. There are many perspectives to a deal, you just need to find the one that fits.

There is no set-in-stone requirement for due diligence, because every business is unique, but there is a standard list of documents that most buyers ask for, including:

- Three years of tax returns
- Profit and loss for the current year and closest completed month with balance sheet
- Profit and loss for the three prior years with balance sheets
- Electronic copy of lease with amendments
- Payroll summary report for all employees with W2s
- Income list by customer or number for B2Bs
- Merchant services summary for prior year (retail)
- Organized bills by category and year
- Copy of the leased equipment, if any

There are many variables depending on the business you're in. I tell sellers to forget they are the sellers and ask themselves what they would want to see to verify the business. While it is important to try to comply with a buyer's requests and to appear transparent, it is equally important to protect your business and your employees. I have some rules regarding due diligence for buyers:

- Buyers are not allowed to disrupt your business
- Potential buyers should not have access to social security numbers
- Buyers should not be able to speak to employees unless the seller approves
- Buyers are not allowed to talk about the business being sold to suppliers, or to related industry vendors
- Buyers cannot stalk the business

Case Study 10.

One of the most perilous parts of a business transaction is the landlord and the lease—although on some other day, I might say one of the biggest potential problems are the third parties we deal with throughout the transaction, because in truth anything can happen.

I could have written a book about landlords and property management alone. In California, it's as if they are superstars and you are the paparazzi bothering them for a minute of their time. I've been here since 1999 so I have lived through the rise in property value in real time. The rents seem to have no limit, and the math gets crazier every year. You must be prepared for the 800-pound gorilla of leasing to be difficult to deal with. It's great when you get a smaller landlord who seems easier to work with, or an individual person, or a commercial/industrial lease space. Industrial is typically the easiest, but even then, you are thrown for a loop every now and then. I was recently asked to sell a business that I had already sold the year prior in an industrial space. It should have been easy. I found a buyer that was perfect on paper: good credit, plenty of liquid capital and 10 years of experience leasing a commercial space.

The only thing this great buyer asked for was a total of five years of lease in almost any combination, which is completely reasonable. Two years and nine months remained on the current lease. I contacted the property management and asked for a lease assignment of the current lease plus a three-year option. They refused, saying that they only do assignments with renewals. I said that didn't really seem to be a benefit to them but sure, ok, I'll take one of those please. Usually, landlords offer options, and they insert the language "fair market value" allowing them to increase the rent to anything they want. This gives them a way to get rid of a bad tenant if it becomes necessary. The buyer that I had for this business had plenty of money, they just wanted more time. The property management would not budge. The buyer offered to increase the lease deposit, they still refused. The buyer offered to pay out the two years and nine months in advance to get another three years added to the lease, they still refused. Sometimes logic doesn't apply, as in this case. In the end we had to make a small concession at our end to save the deal, and it was well worth it. The point of this story is that it is not always easy, even when it should be.

Chapter 7

ESCROW

YOU ARE SELLING YOUR BUSINESS AND YOU'RE WONDERING IF OR WHY YOU should use an escrow company. Well, there are a few reasons why you should:

- Neutral third party to facilitate the money
- Inexpensive peace of mind for both the buyer and seller
- Clear cut-off and restart of liability for both sides
- In certain states, compliance with the bulk sale law

There are reasons that you might be required to use escrow services:

- If the buyer has applied for a loan, most lenders require that an escrow is established.
- If the sale of an alcoholic beverage license is involved, the ABC requires that an escrow is established.
- There are many escrow companies, but most are not experienced with business transactions. Escrow agents that handle business opportunity transactions and bulk sales are highly specialized, as they know the difference between residential and commercial transactions, and when applicable, the know how to comply with the requirements of the bulk sale law.
- In order to make sure the buyer receives clear title to the business and personal property, the escrow agent can order UCC searches and obtain a certificate of release of buyer from the Employment

Development Department, Franchise Tax Board and California Department of Tax and Fee Administration (formerly the State Board of Equalization).

- They comply with escrow requirements of the buyer's lender and the Alcoholic Beverage Control Board.
- Funds are not disbursed until all conditions of the transaction have been met.
- Many states have eliminated the bulk sale law, but California has not. The law was created for protecting a buyer from successor liability for debts that were incurred by the seller. A transaction is subject to the bulk sale law if the sale is not in the ordinary course of the seller's business of more than half of the seller's inventory and equipment. For example, the sale of a gas station is subject to the law, but the sale of gasoline is not, because the gas is sold in the ordinary course of the business. However, the buyer is not required to comply with the law when the business is valued at less than $10,000.00 or more than $5,000,000.00. Typically, the owner of the business orders product for resale and then has 30 days to pay for it. The vendor providing the product is known as the "creditor." When a business is sold, a notice to creditors of bulk sale must be published in a newspaper for 12 business days and re-corded in the county where the business is located (and if different, the county where the seller's chief executive office in California is located) when both of the following apply: (1) The seller's principal business is the sale of inventory from stock (such as a retail store or convenience store), including those who manufacture what they sell, and (2) On the date of the bulk sale agreement the seller is located in California, or if the seller is located in a jurisdiction that is not a part of the United States, the seller's chief executive office is in California. Publication and recording of the notice allows the creditor to file a claim with the escrow agent to make sure any outstanding amount due by the seller is paid at, or prior to, the close of escrow. The date of publication determines the "sale date," which in turn determines the closing date. The close of escrow is on or after the sale date (not before). If the buyer does not follow the bulk sale law, they risk becoming responsible for debts owed

by the seller and/or for the business. Possible debts could be: sales tax, business taxes, unsecured property tax, an equipment lien, judgment lien or superior court lien.

- Allocation of the purchase price. At some point the escrow officer will ask for the allocation of the purchase price. The buyer and seller must agree on the purchase price's definition due to the tax implications on both sides. The entire purchase price will be separated into sections such as goodwill, inventory, franchise value, covenant to non-compete, and fixtures and equipment. A sales tax will be collected by escrow for the value of the fixtures and equipment.

The price of escrow varies depending on the company, but I have found that it is much lower than a residential escrow. Some of my past clients have wanted to use an attorney, and that is an option you should consider if you have special circumstances. If you have many details that need to be specifically written out in an agreement, such as the specifics of a note that is being drawn up, then that portion should be handled by an attorney. However, it is almost always much more cost effective to just use escrow than an attorney for the bulk sale and the lien searches. I have found my professional contacts in escrow to be extremely beneficial in dealing with all the local agencies because they have established relationships with them.

Case Study 11.

I once sold a janitorial company that did commercial window washing. We quickly found a buyer, but the seller had an audit scheduled with the EDD. He was sure that all would be resolved before the close of escrow. The seller was well prepared, he brought four boxes of files to the meeting and was represented by his tax attorney. About four hours later, he called me almost hysterical, saying that the meeting went badly because the examiner didn't speak English well and clearly did not fully understand what they were saying. She just kept saying that the file would be moved up the chain to her superior. But her superior had a stack of files on his desk about three feet thick and he would

---

not get in front of the manager for another two months! We needed to close escrow in seven days or the buyer was going to walk—he made that clear. Desperate, I called my long-time escrow contact and asked her for help. After completing thousands of escrows over 20+ years, you manage to make friends in high places. She was able to get the file moved to the top and negotiated a hold-back, so that the deal would close and EDD would have time to examine the file at their own pace.

It's almost impossible to think of all the things that could happen in a deal, but they do happen. Knowing the very best people to work with is critical in the successful transfer of a business. Could an attorney have done this transfer? Yes. Could he/she have negotiated this outcome? Probably not, and they would be charging by the hour for failing to do so.

Chapter 8

PREPARING FOR A SMOOTH CLOSING

THE MOST MOTIVATING THING I TELL SELLERS IS THAT THE MORE YOU DO
to prepare the buyer to take over without issue, the less they'll bother you
post sale. Running the business has probably become second nature for
you, but what if you dropped off the planet tomorrow, could someone step
in and fill your shoes? SOPs (standard operating procedures) and CRM
(customer relationship management) are both useful tools in ensuring
continuity if you're not around, and both make it much easier for a buyer
to take over.

SOPs could exist in the form of a workplace manual, organized by department. This should be a detailed blueprint of each department's oper-
ation, and the staff members responsible for each specific duty. It should
include protocols used in rare or emergency situations should they arise,
and even who to call if certain items break or stop functioning. This
might seem tedious, but remember that it took you years to gain all this
valuable knowledge and insight. The first time something goes wrong in
the business—and something surely will—do you want the buyer calling
you to complain, or do you want him/her referring to the manual, or list
of persons to call?

CRMs are fabulous tools that allow virtually anyone to pick up where the
last person left off. If you are unfamiliar with this type of program you
will find many low-cost solutions. The key benefit to using a CRM is the
detailed information per client or per contact. It is only a magic bullet

if it's used correctly, with the information having been inputted every time there's been dialogue or contact. Think about all the accounts you have, and the conversations that have taken you to your current position today. Even problems in the past are good to know when you take over a business, so that you can be extra sensitive to them, and ensure that they don't repeat.

If all this is too much for you, then at the very least prepare a detailed list of all the companies that you are doing business with, sorted by business, vendor, or client. Detail the companies that you are doing business with, such as utility companies, landlord, cable, phone systems, software or web hosts, subscriptions, leased equipment, etc.

VENDORS

Make a list of all the vendors you deal with such as suppliers and anyone else you need to run the business, include the account number detail, as often this won't change, even though the ownership has. Sometimes sellers are reluctant to let vendors know that the business is changing hands, but most large companies are savvy enough to know when a business is transferring—due to escrow publication, they will probably find out anyway. It is possible that they might put you on C.O.D. until the deal closes to ensure that they are paid, or they might file a lien. Even though you would prefer to do business as usual, it's better to make them aware. Some companies issue credit to the company, and when I say "company," I'm not necessarily speaking about the corporation, which is also possible. I'm speaking about the goodwill built up between the vendor and you (the business entity). If this is the case, they might feel duped after the sale because of the relationship and take it out on the new buyer, and that's why it's best to be upfront about it. The new buyer might also have to establish their own credit with the vendor; allowing this process to take place ensures that the buyer won't have to suddenly come up with more money for inventory after the financial drain of buying the business. The number two reason buyers fail to successfully run the business they have just bought is being undercapitalized from the start. When you started the business, you had the luxury of learning over time, but they are starting off with the business in full-swing, so they need all the help they can get. In case you're wondering about the number one reason buyers fail, it's an inability to be an entrepreneur, with all that implies.

INVENTORY

In a perfect world the buyer will pay you exactly what you paid for all the stock you have in your business. In the real world I have met business owners who aren't exactly sure how much stock they actually have, or the amount they paid for it. One thing you can do is start organizing your stock into sections and find the cost or invoices for it. If your business has seasonal stock, it can be easy to separate and associate the appropriate invoices with the right stock. You can choose to do the inventory yourself, along with the buyer of course, or you can both elect to hire a company to count the stock for you. I prefer the buyer and seller to do it themselves if it isn't too cumbersome. This gives the seller and buyer a chance to discuss the products and their success in the business, including reordering and trends. If you have old and obsolete inventory, I suggest clearing it out prior to the sale, or be prepared to significantly discount it or give it to the buyer for free. Many of my clients use the opportunity when applicable as in the case of merchandise, to donate their inventory to get the tax credit write-off.

#1 Worker Bee

Chapter 9

EMPLOYEES

FOR SELLERS WHO HAVE OWNED THEIR BUSINESSES FOR A LONG TIME, saying goodbye to their employees is like saying goodbye to family or a dear friend. I have had many sellers who feel guilty about selling, and about the fate of the employees, but remember that they might be dear to you, but they are paid to show up, and they are employees. Nevertheless, it is complicated whenever there is a relationship involved. It took the employees a long time to get used to you and your behavior patterns, and now they will have to get used to someone else, and no one likes that. It's your job to help them see that a fresh point of view might help them to do their job in a better way, and/or that the new owner has plans for expansion, which will give employees more opportunities to advance within the company. You can play an important role in getting them excited for something new, rather than dreading the unknown.

It would be very helpful to the new owner if you prepare a file per employee with all their hire paperwork, contracts, performance reviews, reprimands and commendations. I recommend not telling anyone the business has been sold until the deal is very close to closing or closed. Sometimes that's not possible of course, such as when key management must be informed because they are part of the sale. In most cases of small business sales, it is best to keep it to yourself until the right time. Employees can find the business transfer very unsettling, and they think all kinds of scenarios up in their heads. I strongly suggest you tell everyone at the same time, at the end of escrow. Hold a mandatory employee meeting and tell everyone what an honor its been working with them. Explain that you have decided to sell but you have found a great replacement, and then introduce the buyer right away. The key to a good handover is to make the introduction at the same time, otherwise that active imagination will take over and you could have some trouble on your hands.

Case Study 12.

I once had a flower shop listing that was high volume and quite labor intensive. When I found a buyer and had accepted an offer, I told the seller not to tell any of the employees. She informed me that the manager was a good friend, and she could trust her with information of the business being sold. I asked her if she was paying this good friend a wage and she said she was, "well then, she's not a friend, she's an employee," I replied. She didn't listen to me, which is why this is a story, and the predictable happened. The manager/friend told one other employee who then told two more employees and so on. The problem is that every time the story is retold it gets the opinion, concerns and embellishments of the story teller. It is hard for you to put yourself into the mind of employees. They are very concerned about being fired from their job, so they come up with scenarios that "could" happen. The truth becomes lost in translation, but the buyer needs to retain those employees in order to be sure that the business survives and thrives as it always has. In the case of the flower shop, about one third of the employees quit in fear of losing their jobs to the big bad buyer that was coming, who was "definitely going to bring in all their relatives to replace everyone!" Surprisingly, the deal didn't go south, but it did take us an extra month to close, so the seller could hire and train new people to fill the roles she had lost.

The important take-away from this story is that this is a business, and just as it wouldn't be appropriate to discuss other things with your employees, this is just another subject that they can learn about at the end of the process, when you have the deal closing and you can control the message to all the employees at the same time. It's in everyone's best interest long-term.

Chapter 10

TRAINING

THE EXPECTATIONS OF TRAINING SHOULD BE AGREED UPON AT THE VERY
beginning. Sellers often ask what the norm is and I tell them every business
is unique. I ask them how long it should take a reasonably intelligent person to learn what they do, and the answer always varies. This goes back to
getting your business ready to sell. If you have trained and cross trained the
employees to run all aspects of the business, then the buyer will feel secure
with you leaving. As much as you want to get out, the buyer will figure out
that it's in his best interest for you to leave too. The employees are confused
enough dealing with the "new boss," they are not sure how to treat the old
boss because they habitually turned to them for guidance and approval. I
suggest that whatever has been agreed upon in the purchase agreement is
dealt with in a formal fashion later. For example if you've agreed to train
the buyer for two weeks at 30 hours per week, the training will include the
phone time, the driving to vendors, driving out to customers, time at the
business and so on. It is important to keep a log of what you did that first
week, so you can have it initialed by the buyer after week one. We do this
for two reasons, one is to cover the seller from having any later accusation
that he didn't spend the time that was agreed upon. The second is to show
the buyer that he should pay attention because he has a lot of ground to
cover, and his time is running out.

Larger and more intricate businesses require the seller to stay on for an
extended period, but again, there is no certain answer, as it depends on the
business and the seller's role. It is important to establish early on whether

the time you spend in the business will be included as part of the sale, or whether they will compensate you independently for the time you spend working post sale. I get a lot of questions regarding this subject, depending on the structure of the purchase agreement. For example, the main reason a buyer will ask for a seller to carry back paper is to ensure their involvement post sale if help is needed. My advice regarding training is to be generous. If the buyer does not intend you to remain in the business, then they will most likely tell you to leave even before you are required to do so. However, if you give the impression that you don't want to spend any time with them, they will become suspicious and start questioning your intentions. Buyers do their due diligence in review of the documents and the inspection of the business, but at some point, they must have faith that you, the seller, has been honest, and that they are doing the right thing. If the intention is for you to stay, then you must draft an employment agreement and be able to live with the terms. Some people can't handle not being in charge anymore, but others feel liberated by this. When you own your business, you must be responsible for all aspects of it, and you are the overseer of everything, but there's probably one department that you favor over another. Let's say that you enjoy doing sales, but you have no interest in managing people. An employment agreement with the new owner which defines your role as strictly sales with no other responsibility could potentially get you back to the place that might have attracted you to the business in the beginning. It's normal not to enjoy every part of the business, especially the stress and responsibility of finances.

Chapter 11

CLOSING AND DISBURSEMENT

THIS IS EVERYONE'S FAVORITE CHAPTER IN THE PROCESS AND I PROMISE you, by the time we get here, you'll be ready to start the next chapter in your life. Whether your deal is in escrow or with attorneys, the end is stressful for all parties.

LOANS

In cases where financing from a third party is involved, even more stress is involved! Banks have a bureaucratic method for moving files along and funding loans. After the great recession of 2008, many banks got into trouble for giving loans out to people who weren't qualified; now they are extra careful to be sure that the file is completely filled with all the documents in the checklist. It sounds easy, there's a checklist... let's just give them the documents. The problem is that they don't ask for all the documents they need upfront, and for some reason they ask for them piecemeal. I refer to this as the Columbo method, the fictional Detective Columbo would always say, "Ma'am/sir, just one more thing..." The point is that no one wants to be the person who didn't get something right in your file, so they are very cautious. It takes a lot of diligence on my part to be the gatekeeper in making sure they realize as early as possible what is missing, so the file can move from one desk to another, get the final signatures to go to the closing department, and get funded. Typically, the funds will wire directly into escrow's trust account, or into the borrower's account if escrow is not being used.

ESCROW

As soon as the deal has a definite closing date and the escrow file is complete, they can prepare the estimated closing statement for both the buyer and seller. It is normal for escrow companies to hold back some money if there are any possible liens that might come up later. A good example is the BOE (Board of Equalization), where you pay your sales tax. You can't close your account until you close your escrow, but escrow's primary job is to be 100% sure the business has no liens or debts that the buyer might be responsible for after closing. They typically won't hold back too much, unless the file is complicated, and riddled with problems. Once they get all the official clearances, they will mail/wire you the balance.

BROKERS

Brokers are paid directly from escrow, or from the accounts that have been opened for the buyer's new entities if attorneys are used. Escrow or attorneys should have asked everyone to send in a list of account numbers and banking information for money wiring, with approval from all parties. Getting paid at the end is typical, but there are some cases when some money might have been dispersed along the way, as in the case where a listing required significant expenses, and the broker negotiated for compensation paid by the seller for some of the out-of-pocket expenses. All this should be reflected in the closing statement.

TRUSTS

If you've opted for a trust or some other type of tax saving vehicle, then the funds will go directly into the third-party account that you set up.

CLOSING THE DEAL

Closing typically occurs when all contingencies have been met, and the seller has been paid their consideration for the business. However, there have been cases where the buyer has taken possession of the business, but the transaction hasn't closed. This happens when there are third party reasons that the transaction can't close, i.e. liquor license transfers, availability of signers, licensing issues etc. Having a buyer take possession prior to the deal being closed is not recommended, but it is done. The only thing required is that it must be fully funded, and there must be a valid lease assignment.

Conclusion

In conclusion, selling a business is like navigating white water rapids: full of exciting and sometimes perilous occurrences, but once completed, you are left with a sense of accomplishment like no other in surviving it. If you're tackling the rapids you need the right equipment and the right guide to get you through. The same principle applies when selling your business. Having someone advocate for your perspective and needs to the other side, in a manner that can be appreciated is the difference between a deal being closed or not.

As I said in the beginning of our journey together, choose your team wisely because they are representing your legacy, the business you have spent your life building. The people you hire or don't hire will have ramifications long after the sale, so do it well and exit your business in style.

Selling your business is a big deal, for many of us it's like letting a small piece of your soul go. Do the work on the whole picture of your life, so that you are ready to let it go on to someone else, and you can have your opportunity to try something new. It is not the end, it is the beginning of whatever comes next for you. That could be retirement, it could be a new job, or it could be a new business. The point is that you are now free to try new things, travel, get up late if you want to, spend more time with your favorite people, go back to school, take up a new hobby, whatever you've been putting off, this is your time.

Only you will know when the time is right for you, and my message is simply don't be afraid of the change. Change can be great. You are so much more than the business you've built, and it is probably only one of your many talents.

I'll close with a quote from C.S. Lewis, "There are far, far better things ahead than any we leave behind."

Christina Lazuric Woscoff

www.ingramcontent.com/pod-product-compliance
Lightning Source LLC
Chambersburg PA
CBHW022124170526
45157CB00004B/1744